IMAGES
of England

BIRMINGHAM
WOMEN

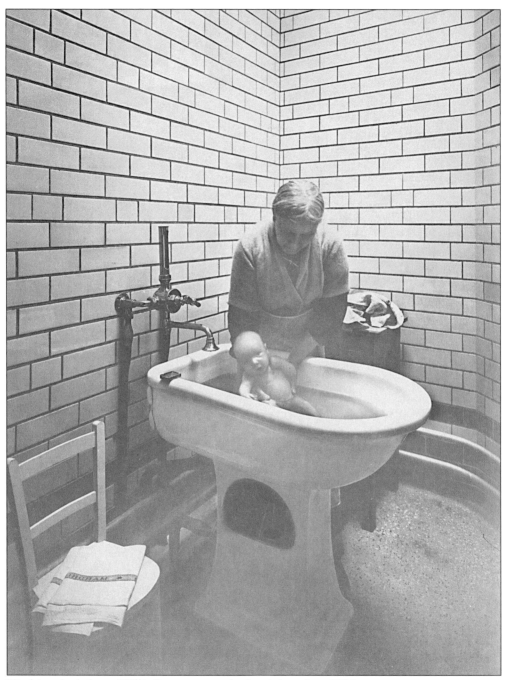

Washing the baby at Willis Street cottage baths, Ashtead, *c*. 1930.

IMAGES
of England

BIRMINGHAM
WOMEN

Compiled by
Margaret D. Green

TEMPUS

Tempus Publishing Limited
The Mill, Brimscombe Port,
Stroud, Gloucestershire, GL5 2QG

ISBN 0 7524 2095 X

Typesetting and origination by
Tempus Publishing Limited
Printed in Great Britain by
Midway Clark Printing, Wiltshire

Testing toys at Chad Valley, Harborne, *c.* 1935.

Contents

Grenade makers at Mills Munitions, Bridge Street West, *c.* 1916.

Acknowledgements

All the photographs, except those on pp. 100 and 106, are from collections held by Birmingham Library Services. I am grateful to Cadbury Schweppes Ltd for permission to use the photographs on pp. 11, 20b, 22-23, and 26-28, from Bournville Village Trust material deposited in Birmingham City Archives. The photographs on pp. 29, 39, 94b, and 122a are also from City Archives; p. 100 is by courtesy of the Kendrick family from a copy in Birmingham Art Gallery; pp. 102 and 103a by courtesy of the Barton family; p. 103b by permission of the Royal Photographic Society; and p. 106 by courtesy of Lyn di Mascio Walton.

Thanks also to Paul Taylor of the Local Studies and History Service, to Peter James, Head of Photography, and to Fiona Tait of City Archives. My special thanks to Susan, Richard and Gavin Abson for their help with the word processor.

Introduction

The photographs in this book illustrate the lives of women in Birmingham from the mid-nineteenth century through to the 1950s and the eve of the modern feminist movement. Their lives were little different to those of women in any other large town in England. Marriage was the expectation and wish of most women, regardless of class. Because the lives of these women centred on their families and homes, they cannot be separated from the lives of children and men. In a society without the safety net of a welfare state, the survival of the family unit and of its individual members depended on mutual support.

Girls helped around the house from a young age, and at ten or twelve could be sent away into domestic service if no longer needed at home. By the 1850s, the workshops and factories of Birmingham were providing alternative employment to domestic work for girls and women who had to earn a wage. In 1841 only 12% of women over twenty worked outside the home. Although by 1901 this figure had increased to 37% of girls over the age of ten, the nature of the work they did remained largely unskilled. Some industries quickly began to rely upon cheap female labour. In 1861, 94% of Gillott' s steel pen workers and 58% of button workers were female. Few however worked in jewellery and gun making – industries which were still regarded as skilled crafts and therefore unsuitable for women. Married women could not work regularly, but when they did they preferred the relative independence of factory work. Photographs taken in factories and workshops show that women workers were there from the beginning, forming a vital part of Birmingham's industrial and economic history.

The role of middle class women was strictly domestic, and until the 1880s, if a woman inherited money or property, it belonged to her husband. However, from the 1860s, many of these women found a role in philanthropic activities, playing an important but hidden part in the life of the town. Political and social awareness had early roots here, invested largely in the non-conformist communities, and the Quakers in particular. The first ever female anti-slavery society was established in Birmingham in 1825, and thousands of local women had supported the Chartists. As the gap between rich and poor became greater, the privileged women of Edgbaston, Harborne and Handsworth involved themselves in causes for women and children less fortunate than they were. They were not just content to serve on committees and raise funds, but went into the factories, slums, prisons and hospitals. No cause was too grim, but there was a lighter side to their endeavours in improving adult education and forming social clubs. They called themselves 'women workers' and in 1887, when the Ladies Union was formed to co-ordinate the different groups, over forty associations were represented. As the National

Union of Women Workers, they founded the Women's Settlement in Summer Lane, which still exists today. Two, three and four generations of Cadbury, Sturge, Kenrick, Southall, Lloyd and Mathews women, and many others, devoted their lives to helping working class women and their families.

In the first half of the twentieth century working women's lives began to change. Social legislation improved their education, health and working conditions. Thousands moved into new municipal housing estates in the suburbs. There was leisure time for dancing and the cinema. Life still revolved around the home and factory work, but with better education many girls now had the chance to become nurses and teachers, and work in banks and offices. By 1926 working women had found a political voice in trade unions, socialism and the co-operative movement. Their experiences in the Second World War were to have a long lasting effect on women's expectations. The year 1948 saw the establishment of the National Health Service, but housing remained a major social concern, with over 25,000 slums as late as 1960. Birmingham was still the City of a Thousand Trades, supported by its women workers. Women still married but there was a growing realisation that domesticity was not the only option. In less than twenty years, the city and its women would be utterly different.

Historically women's lives have been confined by their role as carers, by financial constrictions and by social conventions. However there were always some women who would lead different lives. Middle class women were able to travel, and being educated, could write novels, poetry and worthy tracts. In the late nineteenth century, many, like Mary Lloyd, discovered a vocation in nursing, or teaching. There were always women who successfully ran their own businesses. Often a widow kept up the pub, shop or workshop, which had been run by her husband. In 1818, among Birmingham's confectioners and dressmakers, could be found Alice Pitt, locksmith, Elizabeth Gill, sword-maker, and Lucinda Evetts, brass-founder. Elizabeth Swain successfully traded as a canal carrier at Friday Bridge for thirty years, after her first husband died in 1813. Martha Wooldridge succeeded her husband as keeper of Peck Lane prison in 1799. However the opportunities to be creative were few. Kate Bunce and Georgie Gaskin were rarities, supported by liberal families and an enlightened art school. Above all women were supposed to be respectable but there were those who deserted their families, and took up prostitution and thieving. Ann Bamford, hanged in 1818 for counterfeiting, was doubly condemned for rearing her children into the trade.

Many of the photographs in this collection were taken for social surveys, and as such the working class women, and men, are anonymous. It was easier to locate photographs of working class women at home and at work, than to find photographs in public collections of the middle class philanthropic women. They were firstly the dutiful wives and daughters of politicians and industrialists, and so photographs of them were rarely made public. The few 'women workers' portrayed here must serve as symbols of their whole movement.

The Local Studies and History Service at Birmingham Central Library would be pleased to hear from anyone with photographs of women at home, at work and at leisure, which they think might be of interest. Coverage of the period after 1960 would be particularly welcome as that was a time of great change for women.

Margaret D. Green
July 2000

One
Homes and Families: Contrasts

Girls at St Thomas' School, Bath Row, *c.* 1900. Aged between twelve to fourteen, they could soon be entering the adult world of work, having already spent a large part of their childhood helping out at home.

Court 2, Richard Street, near Saltley gasworks, 1905. Court life was a shared experience; with communal toilets, washhouses and outdoor water taps. In the first half of the twentieth century, most working class people lived in this kind of environment.

View into the court at No. 44 Tower Street, Newtown around 1890. As well as houses, this court also contained a japanning workshop and St Nicholas' church Sunday School. Japanning was a widespread trade in Birmingham, and involved a process of covering metal wares with black laquer or varnish.

Evening meal in a slum property, *c.* 1939. This is one of a series of photographs taken by Bill Brandt over a period of four years for Bournville Village Trust. They recorded living conditions in slum properties in the central districts, comparing them with conditions on new municipal housing estates in the outer suburbs. For women like the one shown in this photograph, life was a never-ending struggle to keep the family fed, clothed, clean and healthy in the face of appalling living conditions and a poor income. (There are more Brandt photographs on pp. 20-23, and 26-28.)

Drawing room at Gilbertstone, Yardley, 1900. This house was owned by a succession of wealthy industrialists such as Richard Tangye. It was packed with fine glass, china, furniture, mirrors and photographs. The large windows overlooked landscaped gardens with views into the three local counties.

A room in a terraced house, Gee Street, Newtown around 1920. This house still had gas lighting. The ropes hanging from the ceiling were used for airing the washing.

Station Terrace, Hill Street, 1905. A short break on the steps of the court houses was often the only relaxation for working class women.

Afternoon tea at the Grange, Erdington, c. 1905. At the home of Sir John Benjamin Stone, the ladies of the family entertained friends on the terrace. Stone was a paper and glass manufacturer, the first mayor of Sutton Coldfield and an important amateur photographer.

The Midland Arcade, Lower New Street, 1905. Middle class women with money and leisure shopped here for the latest fashions.

Great Russell Street, Hockley, 1905. A front room, converted to a small shop which was looked after by a mother, wife or daughter, boosted the family income.

Teenage girls on washing day, Court 6, Hanley Street, Newtown around 1910. Washing day often extended beyond the traditional Monday, and girls, and sometimes boys were kept away from school to help.

Girls at Edgbaston Church of England College, c. 1900. These privileged daughters of wealthy families had servants to do their laundry.

A marriage party in Balsall Heath, *c.* 1905. The bride, Louise Terry, and the groom, Harry Bate, emigrated to Australia in 1911. The seated flower girl on the right was Mary Winifred Neale, who grew up to become a bank clerk with the Municipal Bank.

A wartime wedding at Barnt Green, October 1918. The bride was Irene Austin, the daughter of Helen and Herbert Austin, and the groom was Capt. A.C.R. Waite.

A marriage party at Ward End, October 1930. The family and friends of Olive Kelsall and Sydney Vincent gathered in the garden after the wedding at St Margaret's church.

Studio photograph of Freda and Dennis Ratcliffe, September 1924, taken as a memento for family and friends.

Family grouping in a garden around 1910, though the identity and place are unknown. A delightfully posed study, this is also a rare early photograph of an ordinary garden. The husband was probably a professional man, a doctor, solicitor, or bank manager, who was able to afford a new large terrace house in an expanding and desirable suburb like Moseley. His wife had domestic staff to clean and cook for her, and a gardener too. The woman standing behind her was possibly a governess or a nurse living in.

A cheerful, extended family in Newtown, *c*. 1935.

The Stone family in the garden at the Grange, Erdington, 1912. The man with the large side-whiskers was John Benjamin Stone, with his wife Jane on his right.

Lawford Street recreation ground, Saltley, 1928. Household chores like fetching water from the outdoor tap, or chopping wood, left little time for play. Note here how many children were minding younger siblings.

Street game, Hockley, 1943. With few cars running, street games were safe where no gardens or green spaces existed. This is a rare example, caught by Bill Brandt, of children playing an organized game, possibly a variation of 'freeze'.

A studio portrait of two unidentified Saltley girls, *c.* 1890.

Ashtead children's outing, *c.* 1930. Delta Metals Ltd and the vicar of St Laurence church joined forces here to organize a day out for local poor children. In the decades of depression, unemployed parents readily took advantage of offers of free boots and tea parties for poor children at the local baths, church or school.

The kitchen in a council house, Kingstanding, c. 1941. Part of the Bill Brandt series, this photograph was intended to show the benefits of municipal housing in the suburbs. The kitchen had a hot water facility, a boiler for washing and a compact stove instead of a range. The introduction of more machines and gadgets to help with household chores began to free many women from the tyranny of housework.

Evening meal in a council house, Kingstanding, c. 1941. The kitchen and dinning room overlooked a garden. The provision of gardens was an early concern of George Cadbury at Bournville. They were healthy places for children to play and growing vegetables supplemented the family income. The level of income decided the different standards of living and lifestyles to be found among council tenants. This couple were clearly better off than the Weoley Castle family shown in the Brandt photographs on pp. 26, 27 and 28.

Studio portrait of a Sikh family, c.
1955. Many of the new settlers from
the Indian sub-continent and the
Caribbean visited photographic studios
like that of Ernest and Malcolm Dyche
in Balsall Heath, for portraits to send
home.

Studio portrait of an unidentified
African-Caribbean couple, c. 1955.
Hundreds of Dyche portraits, including
wedding photographs, exist for the
1950s and 60s, but unfortunately
hardly any are identified.

Unknown soldier with wife and child, *c.* 1916.

Teatime in a council house at Weoley Castle, c. 1941. This and the following two photographs are of the same family, and were taken by Bill Brandt. Although conditions were better than in the central districts, deprivation could be still be found on the new estates. These children were clean and tidy but their clothing was well-worn. The walls were distempered and not papered.

The kitchen in a council house at Weoley Castle, c. 1941. Families who transferred from condemned houses were advised by health visitors on hygiene and the use of domestic appliances. The solution to damp washing had still to be found.

Evening in a council house at Weoley Castle, *c*. 1941. Even when relaxing, a mother's work was never done, with socks still to be darned. The rag rug on the floor would have been made on other evenings like this, with the children joining in and no television to distract them.

Two
Out to Work
1850-1918

Women shirt-makers outside John Wormington's shop, Worcester Street around 1895.

Housemaids at the Grange, Erdington, in their Sunday best, 1899. Girls entered domestic service at a young age, working as much as eighteen hours a day. These girls would generally have lived in, and would have had little freedom.

Domestic staff at Dingley's Hotel, Moor Street, 1905. Much of women's work outside the home was simply an extension of housework. Sewing, cooking, laundry work and nursing were learned early in a girl's life.

Cleaning in a pub using a hand-powered vacuum cleaner, *c*. 1910.

Tearoom staff in the Market Hall, *c*. 1910.

Button making at Elliott's, Regent Street, Hockley in 1853. As many as 14 different processes could be involved in making one button. This girl is rolling the edges of metal blanks. A carding girl was expected to stitch 3,600 buttons in one day.

Baking gilt buttons in a furnace to achieve a fine finish. Buttons were mass-produced from cloth, jet, glass, bone, horn and leather.

The pen-slitting room at Hinks and Wells, Buckingham Street, Hockley, 1851. Pen manufacturers were regarded as good employers, allowing a half-day off on Saturdays. In 1866 the 12 Birmingham pen companies employed 2,400 workers, of which only 360 were men.

Ralph Heaton's Mint, Icknield Street, Hockley, c. 1855. Most of the workers were young people aged between 11-18. Girls sorted the coins discarded the imperfect ones, and wrapped the rest in rouleaux. Heaton's made over 10 million coins a year for the world market.

Rag sorters at Smith, Stone and Knight's paper mill, Landor Street, Saltley, 1895.

The bag making room. Paper bag and cardboard box-making were thought to be suitable occupations for women, not physically hard and fairly clean.

At the Daisy Vacuum Cleaner factory, Gravelly Hill, *c.* 1910. The factory produced a wide variety of cleaners, wheel driven and electric, for domestic and industrial use. The cases were made of wood which female workers polished. In this workshop they fitted the leather bellows.

Almost half of the workers were women, with several working in the office. The company was proud of its working conditions, boasting that the workshops were regularly white washed, and the dining and recreation rooms were warm, well-lit and clean.

A girls' geometry class at Waverley Road School, Small Heath, 1895. As the state increased compulsory education, girls could no longer be excluded. Although they were taught the sciences, they were not seriously expected to use them unless they became teachers themselves.

Dressmaking class, 1896. Domestic crafts had equal emphasis.

Teachers at St Clement's School, Saltley, *c.* 1903. The headmistress, Mrs E.M. Wood, is in the centre. St Clement's was one of the many board schools which opened in the late nineteenth century, creating a demand for more teachers.

Teachers at the Church of England College for Girls, Calthorpe Road, Edgbaston around 1900. Established in 1886, it was a private school for the daughters of middle class families.

Harry Clews, manufacturer of brass household goods, with his family and workers at Darwin Street, Highgate around 1910. In small family workshops like this, women could become skilled craft workers. Wives and daughters helped with production or handled the orders. Often the family home was in the same court.

Women making parts for machine tools at the Birmingham Engineering Company, Spring Hill around 1910. This was typical, unskilled mass-production work done by women.

Elizabeth McNab (1850-1947), forewoman at Kynoch's Munitions, Witton, aged about 30. She began work at the age of 12, and at 22 was appointed forewoman of the percussion cap department, (producing a detonator in the end of bullet cartridges). Foremen, or women, were then effectively employers in their own right, subcontracting to the firm. George Kynoch simply indicated how many caps were wanted and left Elizabeth to produce them. By the late 1870s, orders totalling 150 million percussion caps in a year were routine for Mrs McNab. In 40 years she was absent only to give birth to 7 sons and 1 daughter. To judge from her dress, she made a good living in munitions.

Nurses relaxing at the General Hospital, Steelhouse Lane, *c*. 1900. The conservatory led to the

nurses' home and was donated by Sir John Holder, the brewing magnate.

A nurse at Aston Almshouses, Aston Hall Road, *c.* 1890. Florence Nightingale made nursing a respectable profession, so many women took it up. Not all nurses worked in hospitals, employment could also be found in factories, schools and family homes.

Nurses and patients at the Royal Orthopaedic Hospital, Newhall Street, 1897.

Nurses visiting Dennis Road School, Balsall Heath, 1896.

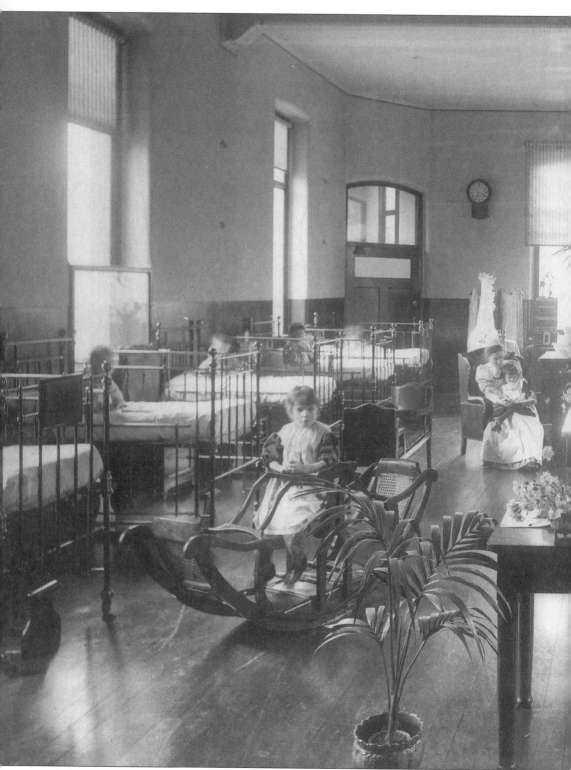

Children's surgical ward at the General Hospital, *c.* 1900. The cots were donated by the

mistresses and pupils of King Edward Sixth High School for girls.

Watercress seller in the Bull Ring, 1901

Flower sellers in the Bull Ring, 1902.

Italian woman selling ice cream in the Bull Ring, 1900. Large numbers of Italians had settled in the St Bartholomew's area by the 1880s. Many were skilled craftsmen but some worked as musicians and hawkers at the market. Ice cream was a family trade in which everyone could help.

Cadbury girls leaving Bournville, *c.* 1900. The workers were then kept strictly segregated, with separate entrances, refreshment areas and recreational facilities.

Workers leaving Kynoch's Munitions, Witton, *c.* 1912. The working conditions and physical environment were vastly different to those at Bournville, where the Cadbury's were benevolent employers.

48

Three
Philanthropy
and Politics

The Women's First Day School, the Priory, *c.* 1890. Since 1848, Quakers in Birmingham had run adult day schools teaching literacy, hygiene, family nursing and other subjects of interest to women.

Mary Showell Rogers (d. 1884). She was founder of the Ladies Association for the Care of Friendless Girls, which aimed to save young women from crime and prostitution. The rescue home set up by the organization was run entirely by women, and although life there was hard, the girls were regarded as victims of social injustice, and not as criminals.

Joanna Hill (1836-1901). She was the niece of Rowland Hill, pioneer of the Penny Post, and her father was the first Recorder of Birmingham. While still in her twenties she became a workhouse visitor and helped to organize foster homes for pauper children.

Girls from the City Mission rescue home, in Noel Road, visiting the Lloyd family at Edgbaston Grove, 1908. The influence of respectable women was considered a vital part of keeping vulnerable girls from straying.

Girls' Club, Street Children's Union, 1920. The Union tried to help neglected children and young adults who spent most of their time on the streets. Educated women of all denominations befriended girls to introduce them to healthy and moral ideas.

Susan Martineau (1826-1894). She was associated for many years with the Homeopathic Hospital, and was a volunteer collector for the Provident Society, which encouraged working people to save. For the Ladies Useful Work Association, she organized an evening recreation room for shop girls.

Mary Badger (d. 1894). Her family was less exalted than that of other charity workers, being millers at Friday Bridge. In 1846, with her friend Miss Harrold, she began teaching blind children at her own expense. She became Honorary Superintendent of the new Institute for the Blind, an office she filled for forty-two years.

Dr Mary Sturge (1862-1925). She was born in Sparkhill, into the famous local Quaker family. Her grandfather had been mayor in 1862, and she was the great-niece of Joseph Sturge, the anti-slavery campaigner. Only the second woman to practice medicine in Birmingham, she was on the staff of the Women's Hospital for many years and was instrumental in the founding of the Taylor Memorial Home to care for the terminally ill. A temperance supporter, she also served on the committee of the Suffrage Society, and worked with Belgian refugees in 1915.

Julia Lloyd (1870 to, *c.* 1940). One of the Lloyds of Farm, Sparkbrook, she was co-founder, with Mrs Richard Gibbins, of the Birmingham Nursery School Movement. The first people's nursery opened in Greet in 1904, in rooms provided by Mr and Mrs Barrow Cadbury.

Julia Lloyd introducing a pet lamb to the Settlement Nursery in 1907. The aim of the people's nurseries was not to offer formal education, but to give small children the home life they missed while their mothers worked.

Mothers' Union outing leaving the settlement in Summer Lane, *c.* 1930. Established in 1899, the Birmingham Settlement was for many years entirely run by women, with its focus on women and children in one of the most deprived areas of the city.

Alice Beale (1845-1940). She was active in women's organizations all her life. She suggested the introduction of women health visitors, and was associated with the Women's Hospital for sixty-three years. She was the first president of the Birmingham Settlement, holding office for twenty-five years.

Catherine Osler (1854-1924). A lifelong campaigner for votes for women, she joined the Birmingham Women's Suffrage Society at the age of fourteen. Middle class and non-militant, it achieved little but kept the cause alive. Under her leadership in the early 1900s, new branches opened, paid organizers were employed and working class women were encouraged to join. She was married to Alfred Osler, the wealthy glass manufacturer and Liberal activist, and was herself president of the influential Women's Liberal Association. For many years she was a vice-president of the local branch of the National Union of Women Workers.

Julia Varley (1871-1952). Born in Bradford, she became a union activist in the textile mills at the age of fourteen. In 1909, Edward Cadbury invited her to Birmingham to organize women's unionism in the city. In 1910 she was one of the organizers of the epic chain-makers strike in the Black Country. She settled in Selly Oak and in 1931 was awarded the OBE for her efforts on behalf of working women. She was the first woman member of the Birmingham Trades Council and as an active suffragist, was twice imprisoned.

Louisa Ryland (1814-1889). Best known as the donor of Cannon Hill and Small Heath Parks, she was a very wealthy woman, with an estate valued at £2,000,000 at her death. She also contributed hugely to the cost of building the School of Art in Margaret Street.

Emma Villers-Wilkes (d.1891). A benefactor of St Philip's church, she paid for two of the magnificent glass windows by Edward Burne-Jones and William Morris. Regarded as an eccentric, she not only instructed that there should be no cattle in the Nativity or blood in the Crucifixion, but also nagged the great duo to hurry up with the project!

Elizabeth Cadbury (1858-1951). As the wife of George Cadbury she was his constant support and companion in his philanthropic work, but this remarkable woman also led a full life in her own right in the service of others. She was involved in a wide range of activities from education, health and hospitals to the YWCA. She was a figure of international status, fortified by her Quaker faith. In a lifetime of voluntary service, she witnessed tremendous changes in the lives of women.

Ellen Pinsent (1866-1946). She was the first woman to be elected to Birmingham City Council, representing Edgbaston Ward, 1911-1913. Her particular interest was the care of damaged children, and for many years she was secretary of the Harborne branch of the NSPCC. Although she left the city in 1913, she continued her work with special schools and the education of disabled and mentally handicapped children. As a young married woman, she enjoyed temporary fame as a budding novelist.

Councillor Ellen Crosskey, in the check coat, talking to voters in Washwood Heath, *c.* 1960. Elected as a Labour Councillor in 1945, she had famous relations – Austen Chamberlain was her uncle, and her father was John Sutton Nettlefold, the housing reformer.

Councillor Doris Fisher, centre right, talking to voters in Soho, *c.* 1960. She was Labour Councillor for Duddeston from 1952, and later held numerous public posts in areas as diverse as women's employment, new towns and the Assay Office. She was created a Life Peer in 1974 and took the title of Baroness Fisher of Rednal.

Edith Wills chatting to neighbours in Rupert Street, Duddeston, 1948. She was the first woman to represent a Birmingham constituency in Parliament, being elected MP for Duddeston in 1945. She joined the Labour Party in 1921, was elected to the city council in 1930, and was active in Cooperative Women's Guilds.

Austen Chamberlain courting women voters at St George's Street public wash house, October 1931. In 1918 only women over thirty were made eligible to vote. It was another ten years before both men and women over twenty-one could vote.

May Day parade in Gooch Street, Highgate, 1956. By 1926, trade unions and the Labour and Cooperative movements were giving women a political and social voice. Women formed a large presence in this parade.

The May Day parades were the opportunity for a diverse collection of organizations to get together, and included communists, suburban Cooperative parties and nuclear bomb protesters.

Marjorie Brown, Birmingham's first lady Mayor in 1974. Born in Small Heath, she was Labour Councillor for the ward from 1954. After 1920, women were more widely represented on the city council, but it was to be a long wait before there was this public recognition of their place in the government of Birmingham.

Four

Hard Lives,
Hard Times

Rag fair at Smithfield Market, 1901. The buying, selling and wearing of second-hand clothes were part of life for the poorest of people.

Blind girls learning to weave baskets at the School for the Blind in Harborne, *c.* 1900. A child with disabilities was often thought to be a disaster in a community when every member of a family had to contribute something to the family's survival.

Deaf girls at the Institution in Edgbaston, *c.* 1900.

Elsie Mellor, Blue Coat School pupil, c. 1907.
Subscribers chose the pupils, who were poor
children or who had lost one or both parents.

Children from the Middlemore Emigration
Homes, 1928. Middlemore children were
rescued from poverty, abuse and undesirable
influences, to be given a new start in Canada.
Children's rescue societies meant well, but
children could be separated forever from
parents, siblings and their extended family
against their wishes.

A Balsall Heath family facing eviction, *c.* 1950. Few people owned their own homes. If illness, death or loss of work occurred, there was no money for the rent. Before the war, it was common for working class families to move frequently to cheaper or better houses, depending on the fluctuations in the family's income.

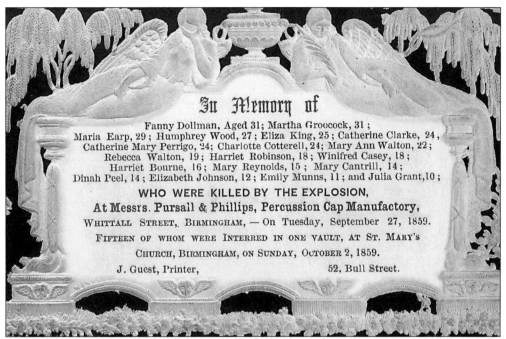

In Memory of

Fanny Dollman, Aged 31; Martha Groocock, 31;
Maria Earp, 29; Humphrey Wood, 27; Eliza King, 25; Catherine Clarke, 24;
Catherine Mary Perrigo, 24; Charlotte Cotterell, 24; Mary Ann Walton, 22;
Rebecca Walton, 19; Harriet Robinson, 18; Winifred Casey, 18;
Harriet Bourne, 16; Mary Reynolds, 15; Mary Cantrill, 14;
Dinah Peel, 14; Elizabeth Johnson, 12; Emily Munns, 11; and Julia Grant, 10;

WHO WERE KILLED BY THE EXPLOSION,

At Messrs. Pursall & Phillips, Percussion Cap Manufactory,

WHITTALL STREET, BIRMINGHAM, — On Tuesday, September 27, 1859.

FIFTEEN OF WHOM WERE INTERRED IN ONE VAULT, AT ST. MARY'S

CHURCH, BIRMINGHAM, ON SUNDAY, OCTOBER 2, 1859.

J. Guest, Printer,   52, Bull Street.

Memorial card for nineteen women and girls killed at work, 1859. The munitions industry, employing mostly women, was a dangerous one. Note that the casualties included girls as young as ten and eleven.

Women and children during the coal strike, 1912. These women in Digbeth had to rely on the Medical Mission to feed their children.

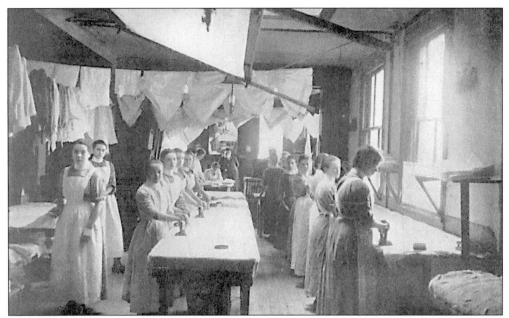

Rescued girls at the City Mission Noel Road Home, 1908. They had to work in the laundry, which financed the home. Laundry work was physically hard, and some girls found that they preferred a lively low life!

Winson Green prison laundry, 1957. Many institutions saved money by having their own laundries. Unwilling inmates were kept occupied, whether the institution was a workhouse, magdalen or prison.

Chopping firewood to sell, 1908. Desperately poor families undertook this kind of home working. The children sold the bundles of wood in the streets.

Carding buttons at home, c. 1906. Carding buttons, hooks and eyes and boxing hairpins were also done at home. In 1906 George Cadbury instigated an exhibition on sweated industries to raise awareness of the exploitation of such workers. Children and sometimes husbands had to help.

Register No. 4.

Name and alias—SARAH GROSVENOR.

Residence—No fixed abode.

Place of business or where employed—None.

Age—60.

Height—4 feet 11½ inches.

Build—Slim.

Complexion—Fresh.

Hair—Brown; Turning Grey

Eyes—Grey.

Shape of nose—Pointed and Indented; Wide Nostrils.

Shape of face—Oval.

Peculiarities or marks—Slight cut right eyebrow; cut scar left eyebrow; cut scar front and side of right wrist.

Profession or occupation—Laundress.

Date and nature of conviction—12th January, 1903. Drunk and disorderly. One calendar month, hard labour.

Court at which convicted—Birmingham City Police Court.

N.B.—Should any known Habitual Drunkard attempt to purchase or obtain any intoxicating liquor at any premises licensed for the sale of intoxicating liquor by retail or at the premises of any registered Club it is requested that the licensed person or the person refusing to supply the liquor will, as soon as practicable, give information of such attempt to the Police of the District, in order that the law may be enforced.

To the Licensee of the ⎱ _Conservative Club Vauxhall Rd_
To the Secretary of the ⎰
Registered Club ⎰ _____

Whose special attention is called to above.

Drink was a comfort and a menace to the working classes. Sarah Grosvenor, at the age of sixty with no home and no work, was on the road to destitution and the workhouse.

Register No. 17.

Name and alias—ELIZABETH THOMPSON, " Hodson," " Nellie Hodgetts,"
" Amy Thomas."

Residence—70, Francis Road, King's Norton.

Place of business or where employed—None.

Age—29. *Height*—5 feet 4½ inches. *Build*—Proportionate. *Complexion*—
Fresh.

Hair—Light Brown. *Eyes*—Grey. *Shape of nose*—Sharp. *Shape of face*—
Oval.

Peculiarities or marks—Slight white scar right cheek.

Profession or occupation—Dressmaker and Prostitute.

Date and nature of conviction—11th March, 1903.   Drunk and disorderly
Prostitute. Fourteen days' hard labour.

Court at which convicted—Birmingham City Police Court.

N.B.—Should any known Habitual Drunkard attempt to purchase or obtain any
intoxicating liquor at any premises licensed for the sale of intoxicating liquor by retail or at
the premises of any registered Club it is requested that the licensed person or the person
refusing to supply the liquor will, as soon as practicable, give information of such attempt to
the Police of the District, in order that the law may be enforced.

To the Licensee of the ⎱ _____

To the Secretary of the ⎰ _____
  Registered Club

Whose special attention is called to above.

Elizabeth Thompson still looked like a respectable woman. Casual prostitution was not an
option for most working class women with families. They valued their good names and the
approval of their neighbours.

BOYD, Elsie Mabel, age 42; Air Raid Warden; of 4 Hugh Villas, Hugh Road, Small Heath. Daughter of Frederick and Mary Elizabeth Hewitt; wife of David Boyd. 10 April 1941, at 4 Hugh Villas.

BRADLEY, Doris Corbett, age 50; of 12 Gladstone Road, Sparkbrook. 19 November 1940, at 12 Gladstone Road.

BRADLEY, Ethel Florence, age 60; of 12 Gladstone Road, Sparkbrook. 19 November 1940, at 12 Gladstone Road.

BRADLEY, Peter John, age 3; of 104 Hansonsbridge Road, Erdington. Son of Alfred William and Lily Bradley. 2 September 1940, at 104 Hansonsbridge Road.

BRADNOCK, Elsie Heath, age 18; of 35 Goosemoor Lane, Erdington. Daughter of Mrs. H. Smith (formerly Bradnock). 10 April 1941, at 35 Goosemoor Lane.

BRADSHAW, Mary, age 56; of 2/34 Trent Street. 10 April 1941, at 2/34 Trent Street.

Entries from the Civilian Roll of Honour for the Second World War. It was the first war that directly involved the whole civilian population of this country.

Bomb damaged houses at Elmtree Road, Stirchley, 12 April 1941. Emily and George Kendrick and their seventeen year old son died here on 10 April.

Cooperative Society float, May Day, *c.* 1920.

Evacuation of children from New Street Station, September 1939. Over 25,000 unaccompanied children left Birmingham in 2 days.

Lench 's Trust Almshouses, Ladywood, *c.* 1912. Some elderly and infirm women without family support were lucky to find a place in an almshouse. For many the workhouse infirmary was their last home.

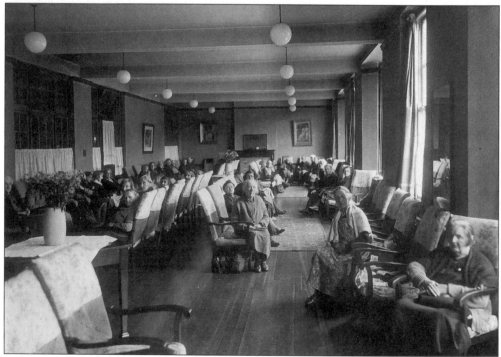

Women at Highbury Old People's Home, *c.* 1955.

Newspaper seller at the General Hospital, 1897. Elderly people had to work for as long as they could. This old lady, known as granny, had as a young girl, been a housemaid at the old General Hospital in Summer Lane.

A blacksmith and his assistant, *c.* 1950. For some, work was a habit as well as a necessity. By the Second World War, the trade of the blacksmith was a dying craft. This smith's wife of many decades knew as much about his work as he did, and would have helped on numerous occasions.

Canal boat women on the Birmingham to Warwick Canal at Bordesley, *c.* 1950. Boatmen were traditionally accompanied by their families. It was a hard way of life and women's health suffered, as did their children's education.

Gypsies at the Black Patch, Hockley, 1898. These Romanies made a semi-permanent home at this site, building a gypsy chapel and cultivating part of the area. They were evicted in 1907 after the death of the elderly Queen Henty, the woman on the left in the long white skirt.

Five

War Work

Voluntary Aid Detachment at the First Southern General Hospital, University of Birmingham, 1916. General service VAD's worked as clerks, cooks, domestics and drivers.

Mrs A.F. Porter, VAD commander at Highbury Auxiliary Hospital, with a new recruit around 1916.

VAD nurses serving dinner in the Great Hall at Highbury around 1916. Many local families, including the Chamberlains, Cadburys, Kenricks and Holders, lent large residences in Edgbaston and Harborne as auxiliary hospitals.

Studio portrait of nurses at Highbury, 1917.
Sister Jorden is on the left.

Kitchen staff at Highbury under the supervision of Miss Lloyd, left, 1917.

Mills Munitions works, Bridge Street West, *c.* 1915. Devised by William Mills in early 1915, the Mills Bomb was then the most effective hand grenade and the safest to handle. This girl was drilling a filler hole in the cast iron body.

The kitchen staff at Mills works, *c.* 1916.

Smoothing the interior of the grenade case before filling, *c.* 1916. The wartime demand for women workers in munitions was very high, and they were well paid. At the end of the war however, most were no longer required.

Checking and packing the finished grenades, *c.* 1916. Over 76 million were used by the allied forces, about half of which were made in Birmingham.

Women's Volunteer Reserve workers at Grove Farm, Erdington, Easter 1916. The WVR was admired because its members were disciplined and keen.

WVR ambulance workers practising to load stretchers, 1915.

Mrs Owen, temporary post lady, *c.* 1916. With most able-bodied men either at the front or in essential war work at home, a wider variety of jobs were available for women to try. Middle class girls, who previously stayed at home, found work in the war hospitals, or as clerks or shop assistants. As domestic staff disappeared into better-paid work in the factories, middle class mothers discovered they were capable of cooking and cleaning for themselves.

A mobile support unit from the first aid post at Grove Lane baths, Erdington, around 1940. Women between the age of eighteen and fifty were expected to volunteer for war work of some kind.

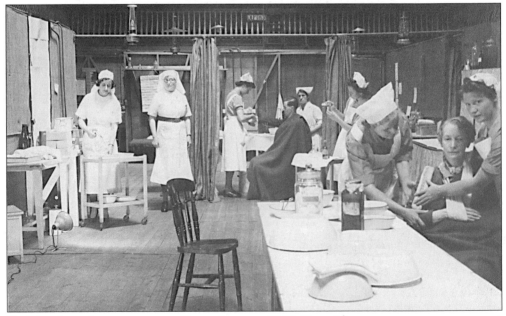

Training for volunteer nurses at Grove Lane, *c.* 1940. First-aid posts were set up to prevent hospitals from being flooded by slightly injured people.

Joan and Moureen welding an armoured vehicle, *c.* 1943. The location is not known but may have been the Metro-Cammell works at Saltley, which was the largest producer of armoured vehicles during the Second World War.

Preparing brass strips for cartridge cases at Imperial Metals Industries, Witton around 1940. By 1939, Kynoch's Munitions works had been absorbed into the metals division of ICI.

Covers for PIAT cartridges on the conveyer belt for gauging, *c.* 1943. The PIAT anti-tank mortar was developed at Witton in 1942.

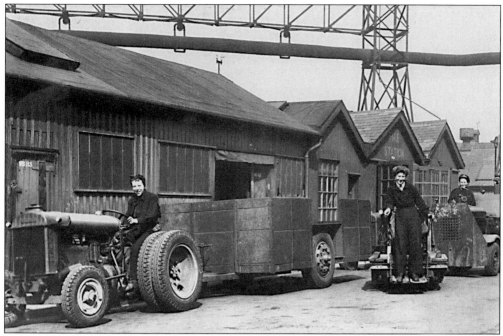

Women driving vehicles at the IMI site around 1943. By 1944 one third of the city's total population was working in the munitions industries.

IMI's contribution to the Warship Week campaign, 1941.

Mounting parts for spraying, Castle Bromwich aeroplane factory, 1943. The factory was built in 1938 in the expectation of war. It began by making frames but became the largest 'shadow' factory in Britain, developing and producing the Spitfire.

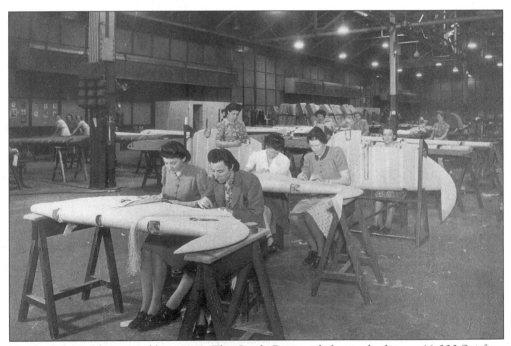

Hand stitching fabric to rudders, 1943. The Castle Bromwich factory built over 11,000 Spitfires and 300 Lancaster bombers.

Land girls at Woodgate, with
Birmetals Rolling Mills in the
background, c. 1943.

Unknown Auxiliary Territorial
Service volunteer, c. 1940. This is a
Dyche studio portrait of one of the
thousands of women who
volunteered for military service.

Girls from W.T. Avery and Co. Mill Lane, Digbeth, in the Win-the-War parade, 21 September 1918. As well as weighing machines, the Avery works produced equipment for testing aeroplane propellers.

Canteen workers from the British Small Arms works, Small Heath, in the Win-the-War parade.

Six
Different Lives

Helen Caddick (1843-1927). Middle class, educated and wealthy, she was an independent woman and travelled the world, keeping detailed accounts of everything she saw.

Lady member of the Smith Street choir at St George's church, Newtown, 1868. For many Victorian women, their participation in church activities gave them a value outside the home.

Cleaning party at St Andrew's church, Bordesley, *c.* 1903. Volunteers ran bible classes and helped with fundraising, but there were also social activities that women could attend, such as evening clubs and excursions.

Double portrait of Mrs Emma Pollard, *c.* 1890. As Emma Hainge, she was a pupil-teacher at St Clement's School, Saltley. She married the Revd Sam Pollard and they sailed for China in 1887 to become missionaries in Yunnan Province. This unusual photograph was produced by precisely overlapping two glass negatives, one of Emma in ordinary clothes and the other of her in Chinese costume. There is a matching study of Sam Pollard.

Catherine Hutton (1756-1846).
The daughter of William Hutton,
Birmingham's first historian,
Catherine kept house for him for
twenty-nine years but still enjoyed a
full life of her own. She travelled
frequently, enjoyed dancing,
collected autographs and fashion
prints, wrote nine novels and over
sixty articles for periodicals.

Mary Ann Schimmelpenninck
(1778-1856). Born into the
Quaker Galton family, she lived
at Great Barr Hall when the
Lunar Society met there. She
turned to writing to make
money, recording her eye
witness account of the meetings
of the most learned men of the
day, Boulton and Watt,
Priestley, Darwin and others.

Female students in the metal shop at the School of Jewellery and Silversmithing, Vittoria Street around 1905. This was a branch of the School of Art, the first municipal school of art in England. A high proportion of the students were female and they excelled at jewellery making, metal crafts, book illustration, and embroidery.

The laboratory at Birmingham Technical School, Suffolk Street, *c.* 1920. After 1918, girls' opportunities to work in science and industry increased.

Alice Coats (1905-1978). She grew up determined to have a career in art. A founder member of the New Birmingham Group in 1933, she achieved fame for her book illustration, watercolours and woodcuts. With the onset of arthritis, she turned to writing about plants, for which she is best known today.

Constance Naden (1858-1889). In her lifetime she enjoyed a considerable national reputation as a poet and philosopher. She studied sciences at Mason College, winning many prizes, and gaining a reputation as a fierce debater and budding feminist.

Georgie Gaskin (1866-1934). Born in Tyseley, she attended the Birmingham School of Art during the period that the school was being influenced by the Arts and Crafts Movement. As a student she won local and national prizes for metalwork and book illustration, but from 1900 concentrated on designing and making jewellery. She was largely self-taught and became skilled at enamelling, a difficult craft to master. This portrait of her in Pre-Raphaelite pose, was taken around 1910 by William Smedley Aston.

Kate Bunce (1858-1927). With her sister Myra (1854-1919) she attended the Birmingham School of Art in the 1880s and 1890s. She achieved fame as a painter in the Pre-Raphaelite style. Some consider her best work to be the church paintings in which she expressed her religious and spiritual nature. Much of her work has disappeared from public view, but 'Melody' and 'The Keepsake' can be seen in the Birmingham Art Gallery.

Myra Bunce, left, with Kate on the right, both in mid-Victorian costume at the Lord Mayor's Fancy Dress Ball at the Council House, February 1914. The sisters came from a wealthy liberal Edgbaston family, which encouraged their early artistic and literary interests. Myra was an accomplished landscape painter and talented designer, specialising in metal work. They worked together on commissions for local churches, with Kate producing the paintings, and Myra the decorative metal surrounds.

Emma Barton (1872-1938). The most famous lady photographer of her time, she took up photography to record her family and was largely self-taught. Born in Digbeth, she was the daughter of a railway porter, and married a local solicitor. She first exhibited her work around 1901, and achieved successes in competitions and exhibitions in Britain, Europe and America. This is probably a self-portrait and dates from 1911.

Most of Emma Barton's work consisted of portraits and allegorical studies of herself, her family and friends. This photograph, with the Pre-Raphaelite theme of the woman and lost love, was entitled 'My Sweet Highland Mary' and dates from 1912.

Her early studies of Madonna and child have been described as among the classics of photography. This one, 'the Awakening' of 1903, won the Royal Photographic Society medal.

Betty and Peggy, the Swing sisters, *c.* 1935. Over the decades the Dyche Studio photographed many clients who were pursuing a stage career.

Dyche Studio publicity shot of Betty Barnes Debutantes, *c.* 1955. Betty Barnes Dance School was next to the Station Hotel in Kings Heath High Street, 1950-1962.

Restoration ladies in the Pageant at Aston Park, July 1938. Organized to commemorate Birmingham's centenary as a borough, over 8,000 amateur performers were involved, orchestrated by a female Pageant Master, Gwen Lally.

Edith Wynne Mathison (c. 1873-c. 1953) She was once the most famous actress to be born in Birmingham. She began as an amateur in musicals and became Henry Irving's last leading lady. She and her husband, Charles Rann Kennedy, were very influential in the American theatre.

The Saglione sisters from San Vittore, Italy, *c.* 1900. Maria, on the right, enraged her family and community by eloping with Giuseppe Saracene from Casino. They came to Birmingham and got married at St Michael's church in Carrs Lane, in 1890. They kept a coffee shop in Coleshill Street and had four daughters and one son. Her great granddaughter, Lyn di Mascio Walton of Sutton Coldfield, is her first descendant to have visited San Vittore.

Afternoon out at Cannon Hill Park, *c.* 1955. As housework became physically less demanding, leisure time increased for many women. Washing machines and vacuum cleaners were wonderful inventions!

Teenage girls enjoying the park, *c.* 1955. Their experiences and opportunities were vastly different to their counterparts, fifty or one hundred years before, and to the girls of today.

Pub party, *c.* 1938. For many older working class women, a Saturday night out at the pub with family and friends was a welcome break from the home.

City office worker enjoying a quiet lunch break in Chamberlain Place, *c.* 1950.

Seven

Out to Work
1919-1960

Girls from Smith's Crisps factory at Tyseley, c. 1930. The food industry was traditionally a big employer of female workers.

Waitresses about to serve tea at the opening celebrations for the Salvage Works at Rotton Park, 1932.

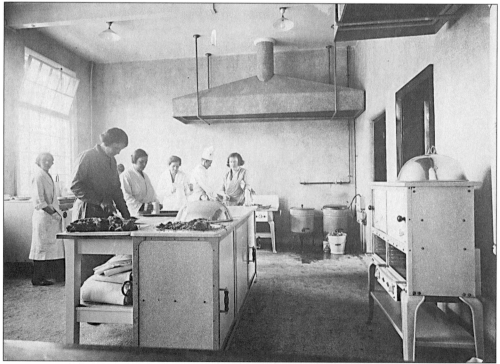

The kitchen staff. Birmingham City Council became the largest employer of manual and non-manual staff, with most workplaces having their own canteens.

Library assistant with the book exchange service, 1929. As many employers did at that time, the city council terminated a girl's employment on marriage.

Ledger staff at the Weights and Measures Department, St Martin's Lane around 1920. With increasing responsibilities in areas such as education, housing and public health, the city council required an army of clerical staff to back up the front line services.

Mabel Harris outside her tobacconist's shop, Weaman Street around 1930. Shop work has been a traditional occupation for women for over two centuries. In 1777, as well as there being numerous grocers, there were women chemists, china dealers, gingerbread sellers, drapers and publicans.

Girls at Sparkhill Junior Commercial School, Stratford Road, 1932. They learned shorthand, typing, filing and basic office skills. Clerical work was considered to be far superior to factory work.

Machinists at Wolseley Motor works, Drews Lane, Washwood Heath around 1935. Women in factories were still largely confined to unskilled work and were paid accordingly.

Feeding sheet metal into the enamelling machine, Parkinson Stoves, Stechford around 1935. Technical advances in the early twentieth century automated many heavy industrial processes. More and more workers supervised machines.

Parkinson works outing, c. 1935. The woman in the white coat was Ada Merrett, the welfare officer.

Switchboard operators at Telephone House, Newhall Street, 1956. Technical innovations added to the variety of work that was considered suitable for women.

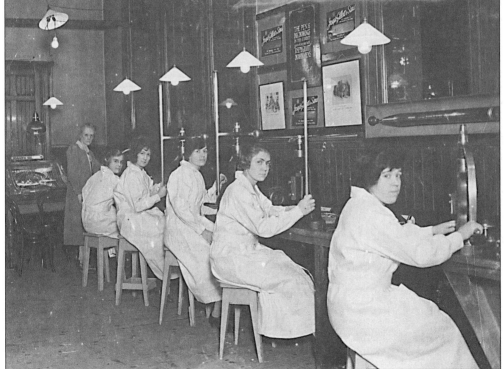

Gillott's staff demonstrating nib-stamping machines at the Birmingham and Midland Institute, 1926. The supervisor, Clarry Greenway, had worked for Gillott's pens since before 1915, when she was first paid a weekly bonus in recognition of her skills.

Inspection of a publican's measures, *c.* 1960.

Barmaid testing a glass-washing machine, *c.* 1960.

Cinema usherettes from the Savoy, Pershore Road, Stirchley, 1932. Mildred Coles, on the left, was the Savoy's first usherette. She sent this photograph to her 'Dear Aunt Jinnie'.

District nurse outside the Bordesley Nurses Home, Moseley Road, 1930. The idea of home visits to the sick poor by trained nurses dates from the 1860s, when Timothy Kenrick paid for a nurse in Ladywood. Mrs W.J. Beale started the Birmingham District Nursing Society in 1870, and Alice Beale, Kenrick's daughter, founded the first home for district nurses. In 1908 there were 8 nurses at Moseley Road, who paid almost 40,000 visits in the course of a year.

Miss Sherlock serving tea at Erdington Cottage Homes, *c*. 1950.

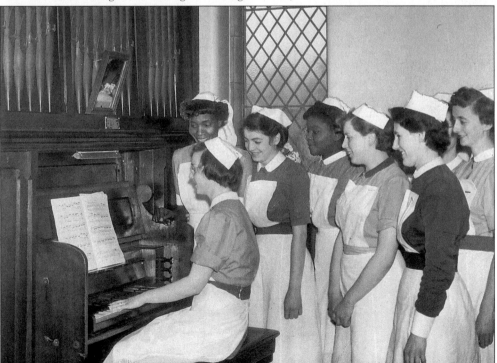

Nurses at the Accident Hospital in Bath Row, 1956. Staff Nurse Campbell was trying the new organ in the chapel.

Making dollies at the Chad Valley works, Harborne, *c*. 1920.

Packing board games, *c*. 1920. The original company made stationers sundries, and after moving to Harborne in 1897, turned to board games.

Checking the strings, *c.* 1930. The firm took its name from the Chad, a small stream running close to the new factory. The girl here was very young, but the boy was even younger.

Girls enjoying a new word game, *c.* 1930. Chad Valley toys were loved by generations of Birmingham children, and their parents!

Thomas Winkles jewellery
workshop in Vittoria Street,
Hockley, c. 1920. This firm
specialised in making chains.
Women workers were usually
restricted to polishing, packing
and chain making; the skilled
work was for men.

Spoking wheels on BSA
bicycles, Small Heath, c. 1950.

At Mitchell Bossley Ltd, gunstock makers, Little Shadwell Street around 1960. Gun making traditionally excluded women. This lady, believed to be Mrs Pavey, was a rare exception.

Throughout the nineteenth century, there were a few women who had their own gun and jewellery making businesses. They were generally widows who had learned the trade while helping their husbands.

Boxing King George chocolates at Cadbury's Bournville, *c.* 1930.

Policewomen in the duty office at Steelhouse Lane station around 1955. The first policewomen, only two, were appointed in 1917 as a temporary wartime measure. By 1935 there were seventeen women on the Birmingham force.

On parade outside the General Hospital, *c.* 1952. In 1950 there were thirty-five women police officers in Birmingham, with duties restricted to the care of vulnerable women and children, clerical work and shoplifting cases.

Cardboard box making at the Birmingham Box Company, Hampton Street, Hockley, 1951.

The London Aluminium Company, Witton, *c.* 1955. Traditional manufacturing was still the basis of the local economy, but within twenty years the 'City of a Thousand Trades' would be changed beyond recognition.

Unknown bus conductress from the Caribbean, *c.* 1960.

Dot Anderson, bus conductress, 1953. Contrary to popular belief, only a small number of women were ever employed on public transport. The 'clippies' were much missed, always happy to give directions and change, and keep the passengers in order!

New shoes! Staff and customers in Day's shoe shop, New Street around 1950.